Athletes Instruction Book

Mazz Marketing, Inc.

© 2006

Wayne Mazzoni

Dedicated to...
My Family

Introduction

Over the course of my twenty-five years as an athlete and coach, I have learned a great deal about what sports means to those that play it. Yet so often we get wrapped up in our practices and games that we don't see the big picture of what sports should mean to us. Some of the thoughts in this book are things I wish I did during my playing career, some are rules I now live by, and others are observations I have made as I have tried to lead and coach young people. If you gain anything from even one of these tips, I will be satisfied that the message has reached you.

1. Only sports and music have Hall's of Fame.

2. Never, ever bet on sports while you are a player.

3. You are what you repeatedly do.

4. For us athletes, sometimes we think a lot clearer when we move. Try to walk and study at the same time.

5. If you don't put much into the team, the losing won't be that bad…nor will winning be that good.

6. Make it a skins game…win each possession, each half, each inning, each hole, each period.

7. You won't regret trying your hardest.

8. Your coach makes recruiting calls to replace you.

9. Be proud in victory, but humble. Other great achievements are happening all over campus.

10. Be your team's student athlete advisory committee (SAAC) representative.

11. Develop a relationship with your schools athletic director.

12. Know your school president on a personal level.

13. If you get cut, ask to be a student manager or coach.

14. Each day you truly get better or worse.

15. The season is 365 days a year.

16. Become friendly with an alumni athlete.

17. Donate to the program after you graduate.

18. Organize an alumni event to raise money. You'll help the team and meet people who can help you after you graduate.

19. 75% of college athletes don't play four years. Be in the 25%.

20. Don't choose a college just for the athletic program.

21. Transferring colleges as an athlete is tough. Take the time to get it right the first time through.

22. Treat team equipment as if it were your own.

23. No matter how good you are, you couldn't have done it without your teammates.

24. Find out who your athletic building is named after and write him or her a personal note.

25. Watch a game of every other team at your school.

26. No matter how good or bad your weight room, you'll find working out comes from within.

27. Jog through campus.

28. Eat smart and in moderation. It will pay off now and the rest of your life.

29. Watch SportsCenter only once a day.

30. Write a journal about your team experiences.

31. Be in your room at lights out time.

32. If you hit it back to the pitcher, fly down the line.

33. When shaking hands after the game, tell the other players who impressed you.

34. Remember you always represent your team, coach, and school.

35. After you graduate write a personal thank you note to the trainers.

36. Less then 1% of college athletes turn professional.

37. Buy your jersey after you graduate. Frame it.

38. Raise money by selling hats, t-shirts, raffles, and ads in a program or media guide.

39. Wear team gear and ask for donations at the local mall or supermarket.

40. <u>Everyone</u> wants to work in sports. If you are serious about a career in sports, work in your athletic department or for a sports organization in the summer.

41. If possible, arrive before and/or stay after every practice.

42. Don't let the team stop at fast food restaurants after games.

43. Take advantage of tutors.

44. Lift weights for the body, read books for the mind.

45. Make sure you are the student in student-athlete.

46. Lead a study hall group for your team.

47. Watch Field of Dreams once a year.

48. Watch Hoosiers once a year.

49. Watch Remember the Titans once a year.

50. Watch Miracle once a year.

51. Nothing is more true then perfect practice makes perfect play.

52. Don't be afraid to offer your coach suggestions on how to improve the team. Just make sure you do it in a meeting, never at a practice or in a game.

53. Give back to the campus or community who supports the team.

54. Write a thank you letter to your high school and summer coaches. Keep them posted on your progress.

55. Get a school hat or shirt for your parents and mail it with a thank you card.

56. Grades come before athletics. Don't let anyone mix these priorities.

57. Don't participate in anything which breaks NCAA rules.

58. Leave the program better then when you arrived.

59. Never ever under any circumstances ruin your life by taking steroids.

60. Know the difference between hurt and injured.

61. Practice with pressure so that you can handle it in the game.

62. All games are big games.

63. It is hard to breathe deeply and feel pressure at the same time.

64. Be happy for your teammates.

65. If not in the game, don't waste time just blabbing. Study the game, learn, and try to help your teammates and coaches.

66. Treat umpires and officials with respect. Without them, you have no game.

67. Drugs and sports never mix.

68. Generally things are never as good or as bad as they seem.

69. Treat all coaches, assistants and volunteers included, with the same respect you do the head coach.

70. An hour of sleep before midnight is like two after it.

71. Learn to party in moderation.

71. Binge drinking can kill you.

72. The best way to change your role on the field is to improve your effort off of it.

74. Be involved in your schools intramurals. Enjoy playing a sport just for the heck of it.

75. Learn golf. It will be the sport that stays with you the longest in life.

76. Learn to communicate with your coach.

77. Help your coach know about good players at your high school or in your area.

78. Get the coaches a gift at the end of the season.

79. Make a team CD for the locker room.

80. Don't view team trips as a time to go crazy. Lots of work took place to make the trip happen.

81. Don't let your team travel by van. Raise money if you must, but upgrade to busses.

82. Find a way to play your sport in the summer.

83. When in college, don't let a job interfere with your development as an athlete. You will work most of your life, but only get four years of collegiate sports.

84. Work on what you are both strongest and weakest at.

85. Try swimming or waterpolo for conditioning.

86. Make a few friends that are not athletes.

87. Drop off extra game tickets to charities.

88. Adopt a local misfortunate child and make them a part of the team.

89. Play video games, but not at the expense of sleep or grades.

90. Go watch a school play or music performance. There is much more to school than sports.

91. Thank the cafeteria staff after a good meal.

92. Always attend the athletic department banquet.

93. Never quit until the game is over.

94. Be self-motivated & low maintenance.

95. Park where you should. Athletes don't get special privileges.

96. How hard you work when no one is around determines how you play when everyone is around.

97. Find the hardest working player on the team, train with him/her.

98. Find the smartest person on the team, study with him/her.

99. Find the more fun person on the team, hang out with him/her.

100. After working as hard as you can, take the time to relax and enjoy your effort.

101. Take lots of pictures in your uniform, you will want to see them years later.

102. Take pictures of your teammates and put them in their lockers.

103. Never forget that Michael Jordan got cut in high school.

104. For all but .001% your education will take you further then your athletics.

105. Be single minded on your goals, but open to all ideas.

106. There are few answers without questions.

107. Wayne Chrebet played years in the NFL, primarily because his Dad sent video of his games to all the NFL teams.

108. Wayne Chrebet also played years in the NFL because he was tough, talented, and driven.

109. Respect your cheerleaders, they work just as hard as any athlete.

110. Be nice to all athletic secretaries for a few reasons; 1) Just because you should, 2) Your athletic experience is better because of their work, 3) They will return the favor when you need it most.

111. Buy personal items with your schools logo. Mouse pads, water bottles, hats. If your school bookstore does not carry them, you can have them made cheaply at many places.

112. You will find great pleasure by training in nature. Run a trail, climb a mountain, jog a beach.

113. Always strive for perfection, but don't expect it.

114. Learn the trait of optimism. It will carry you as far as any other skill.

115. The more powerful the opponent, the more sweet the victory.

116. Study group and team psychology.

117. What you do, not what you say, shows who you are.

118. You can't change your whole life or game at once, but you can certainly change one aspect of it at once.

119. The best things to practice are what you do best and worst.

120. If you want your coach to trust you to do bigger things, first show her you can do smaller things.

121. If you want to lead others, first lead yourself.

122. Remember the quote by William Feather. "Success seems to be largely a matter of hanging on after others have let go."

123. The more you work the more opportunity you will get.

124. Adversity is when you find out about yourself.

125. Be careful trying to please too many people.

126. Your input most likely will equal your output.

127. Think of all games like exams, and then ask yourself if you have studied enough.

128. If you want to sleep well at night and have no regrets when you graduate, the best thing you can do is work as hard as you can right now.

129. If you have big goals you want to achieve, divide it into small tasks to make it reachable.

130. The most important critic is in the mirror.

131. The best way to start any task is to think of where you want to be at the end.

132. Realize that there is no such thing as failure. It is only feedback on the way to your goals.

133. Don't be afraid to change your major, life is often a trial and error process.

134. Learn to tune out all outside factors during a game. The weather, field, fans, officials, etc. They have very little factor in the outcome.

135. If you want to know the difference between first and last, watch a track event. Seconds and inches are often the difference.

136. The first step is often the hardest. If you get to the gym, the workout is usually a good one.

137. Body language is more important then you would think. If you show the way you feel, your coach, teammates and opponents will soon know.

138. Many athletes have issues with their coaches. Just remember, they have been doing their job a long time and most likely are right in what they are telling you.

139. As soon as you say you can't, one thing is sure. You can't.

140. Good habits are just as easy to create as bad ones.

141. Workout, practice, and play as if each time will be your last.

142. If not now, when?

143. With the exception of a few situations, excuses simply get in the way of real learning.

144. Play it one pitch, shot, play, second at a time.

145. Think more about playing the game the right way then about winning.

146. Fundamentals. Keep it simple.

147. If you like the results you are getting, continue what you have been doing. If you don't like the results...

148. If you know what you are supposed to be doing, do it.

149. Never forget that playing sports is a privilege, not a right.

150. Your sport must be your passion. When you lose that, time to do something else.

151. Nothing good will come in an instant.

152. If you can't find the circumstances you want, make them.

153. Learn to visualize. You can practice your skills, your plays, and your performance under pressure this way.

154. On the way to pursuing the best that you can be, you may lose some people. The average person does not have the drive to become the best.

155. While not every part of athletics is fun, you can turn almost any endeavor into more fun. Running on the treadmill might be boring, but jogging a hill with your teammate, overlooking the town might be great.

156. If music inspires you to be better, listen. If books inspire you to do more, read.

157. Fueling up (what you eat/drink) and recovery (rest/sleep) are as important as the energy you spend (practicing/playing).

158. Go watch the pros in person.

159. More often then not, you will become what you think. This can be good or bad.

160. Don't confuse sports (a game) with war (life an death). The field is no place for fighting.

161. No one wants an injury. But it is an opportunity to learn many things about yourself.

162. What you will miss when your career is over is the camaraderie and the focus on a goal.

163. Remember when you win, someone else loses. Be a good winner.

164. Make sure your coach only has to ask you once.

165. You can practice almost every skill in your sport by yourself.

166. With just one other player you can practice every skill.

167. If you find yourself bored, then you simply don't have (high enough) goals.

168. The more you know what you're doing, the less pressure you will feel.

169. "The dictionary is the only place where success comes before work." - Arthur Brisbane

170. Some can be great in a given moment, but consistent performance is more important.

171. Somewhere right at this very moment, someone is pushing themselves to their limits to be the best they can.

172. Details. People trip over little rocks, not big ones.

173. In the end, your effort is the only thing you have control over.

174. Write down your goals, they have a much better chance of coming to life.

175. No one owes you anything.

176. Memories are best when earned.

177. Avoid eating anything heavy after 9:00.

178. Each day, each second is new. You can choose what you want to become and shed your past.

179. Be right for the moment. Crush your opponent, be nice to your girlfriend's dad.

180. Make sure your goal is your goal. Not your parent's goal.

181. Be happy when you get a uniform.
     Happier when they retire it.

182. In general the more one brags, the less
     confident they are.

183. Learn to ask and listen more then you
     talk.

184. Whether or not you know it, you are a
     role model to children.

185. Charity begins at home; help a team-mate in need.

186. Everyone dies, make sure you live.

187. The only thing we know is going to happen is death. So live while you can.

188. Leaders may often be wrong, but they always lead.

189. Root for players, not uniforms.

190. Courage is overcoming your fears.

191. Success is living your life your own way.

192. With the exception of a few things, almost anything you want in life, you can get. The path is simple, decide what you want and constantly work towards achieving it.

193. The sweeter it is to achieve the harder it is to reach.

194. If you are not getting better today, you are getting worse.

195. You have nothing more important then your time.

196. I know you are blessed because you are able to read this.

197. "I can't believe that we would lie in our graves dreaming of things that we might have been." - Dave Matthews

198. Learn from your past, live in the moment, dream for tomorrow.

199. Instead of thinking that you need more, think about doing more with what you have.

200. You can't cram in sports.

201. If you hit bottom, bounce back up.

202. Everyone eventually crosses the finish line, winners just find a better way to get there.

203. If the road to success had no bumps at all, it would not be so sweet to reach the destination.

204. Once you have done your very best, what others think of you is irrelevant.

205. Most often your opponent will try to do to you what they don't want done to them.

206. Experience is easy to gain, but hard to use.

207. It is your own job to increase your motivation and will to win.

208. If things run smoothly, you have one hell of an organized coach.

209. Get busy busting your butt or get ready to be replaced.

210. You will work from twenty-one to at least sixty-five. Enjoy sports while you can.

211. Soon enough you will have no room-mates, advisors, counselors, professors, residence advisors or coaches pushing and caring for you. The sooner you grow up, the better off you will be.

212. Drink water over every other product when you can.

213. If you are unhappy with any aspect of your athletic experience, come up with a way to fix it. This is how the world moves forward. It can also make you rich. Under Armour was started by a football player who couldn't find the right fitting shirt.

214. It seems to make sense that the best way to get better at your sport is to play your sport.

215. The best way to be remembered is as the person who gave her all.

216. Have a plan. Very little good happens by accident.

217. As far as I know, you have to climb to get to the top of the mountain.

218. Choose to be optimistic.

219. Often your most important choice is your choice of attitude.

220. What happens to you only matters based on what happens within you.

221. Since most educators believe that you will become what your expectations are, it only makes sense to raise your expectations.

222. As a college student, you might have empty pockets, but now is the time to fill your heart and head!

223. What would you change if you KNEW you would not fail?

224. If you knew you were dying, what would you change? The news is, you are dying. Change it now.

225. Get a key to the weight room or gym.

226. Often pursuing greatness will separate you from the rest, since most want to be mediocre.

227. The best advice I ever got was that you can choose how to react to anything that happens to you.

228. As Henry Ford said, whether you think you can or you can't, you're right.

229. College can be tough, but don't confuse it with work.

230. Hard times always pass, so learn what you can when your are in them.

231. Just get started, do something. Once you decide to do it and get started, your best will come out.

232. How do hikers climb Everest? A step at a time.

233. Don't tell your coach what you are going to do, do it. Actions speak louder then words.

234. Full effort is winning.

235. Create good habits.

236. The only constant is change.

237. Accept your situation or your ability to change it.

238. If you want your team to change in some way, be that change.

239. For good or bad, your habits will determine what you become.

240. If you want to quit at the end of the season, fair enough. Never, ever, quit during the year.

241. Mike Singletary: "Do you know what my favorite part of the game is? The opportunity to play."

242. Much of coaching is correcting mistakes.

243. A great drill, turn negative thoughts into positive ones.

244. It helps to think of yourself not as you are, but as you can become.

245. Success isn't permanent, at least not without work.

246. Three ingredients to excel; talent, hard work, and will to compete.

247. Bobby Knight was right; "Most have the will to win, few have the will to prepare."

248. You're in or out, no in between.

249. The more you dream, the more you do.

250. There is always a market for the best.

251. You may not be perfect, but you can seek excellence.

252. Pursue excellence for its sake alone, not to satisfy anyone else.

253. Done well, athletics is the most important of all majors.

254. Sports will make you a better parent, spouse, employee, or employer.

255. Run….because you can.

256. Read a great book on the stairmaster.

257.   Do everything in the moment.

258. You will remember the moments more then the details.

259. When you do the things you need to do without being told, you have arrived.

260. The more you want to do it, the less it feels like work.

261. Want to know how this book was written....one tip at a time.

262. If you are not going to do everything involved with your sport, to the absolute best of your talent and effort, then you really should ask yourself why you are doing it at all.

263. You should be smarter today then yesterday.

264. Don't just be better than someone else, be better than your previous self.

265. Yes, this is Heaven.

266. Soon you will learn the best things in life are free.

267. During two-a-day football camp, nothing beats a meal, a shower, and a nap.

268. Do not expect any one, other then you, to make you happy.

269. The less you complain and the more you do, the better things will be.

270. Try to make common sense more common.

271. The only real failure is not trying.

272. It usually takes about two years to be an instant success on the field.

273. Your life must be in balance, being great on the field, but in trouble off it, will eventually take its toll.

274. If happiness in life is a wheel and the spokes are health, academics, family, friends, sports, fun, etc., if one spoke is broken, the wheel does not turn.

275. The best friend you can ever have is yourself.

276. You only have so much energy, make sure you spend it in the right way.

277. Ask why not, instead of why.

278. Be concerned with what you can control, the rest is wasted energy.

279. What you consider the worst time in your life, will soon be a distant memory.

280. Never litter. And don't allow anyone to do it as well.

281. You don't have to become a trash professional, but it won't kill you to pick up someone else's mess now and then.

282. The more you admit your mistakes, the less others will have to tell you about them.

283. You can't rush a rose to bloom.

284. You can't achieve much without a zest for your goal.

285. Call your mistakes, "experience."

286. Call your problems, "challenges."

287. You must learn to say no.

288. Be early.

289. Be happy with what you have, while always striving for better.

290. Someday soon you are going to realize how good you had it right now.

291. Your goal in life should be to enjoy it.

292. The toughest part of any task is the first step.

293. Tom Hanks had to start somewhere.

294. No one else can be you and you should never be someone else.

295. Play hard.

296. Always shake hands after the game.

297. Treat anyone that works on campus as if they were a relative.

298. Treat fellow students as if they were a brother or sister.

299. Judge people inside out, not the other way around.

300. Judge not, lest you to be judged.

301. You can't control the weather, so don't let it control you.

302. If you want change, change the thing or your approach

303. Listen to audio books in your car or portable.

304. Soon, you will add up to your choices.

305. Sometimes, players will eventually hire their coaches.

306. We all have challenges in life, all of us, regardless of money or status, it's a matter of how you face them that makes you.

307. Response-a-bility. You can choose your response to anything in this life.

308. Music > heart < sports

309. One day your kids will ask you about your athletic days.

310. One day your grandchildren will ask you about your college days.

311. Better to have great motivation with a poor gym, then the opposite

312. Practice in the rain.

313. It's okay to not know, but then you had better find out.

314. Bring back sportsmanship.

315. When not in the game, stay in the game.

316. Recipe for success: one part talent, one part determination, one part competitiveness.

317. Most clichés are true.

318. Some day science will fascinate you.

319. In the big picture of the history of the universe, your time on earth is so small it would not register on any time scale.

320. Some freshmen act like seniors, and some seniors like freshmen.

321. Don't do anything just to get it done, stay in the moment the whole time.

322. If you stop a sport, start an instrument.

323. You can always find help…you just have to ask.

324. Think of what you have, not of what you don't.

325. Pipe down and play (when in doubt, shut your mouth).

326. The meek don't inherit the Earth.

327. Some of you can play several positions, some of you who play several positions, can't play one.

328. You can always increase your athleticism.

329. Just because it worked in high school doesn't mean it will work in college.

330. Players are often most ready to be coached after failure.

331. You will make millions of choices in your life, two, maybe three, will direct the path in a significant way.

332. For many of you, some day, sports may not mean all that much.

333. What's your motivation?

334. Turn off the TV.

335. Give or take, college life is about 1000 days.

336. Don't sink all your money into a car when in college, plenty of time for that later.

337. Your average working adult has the following bills to pay: mortgage, homeowners insurance, car payment, car insurance, television, phone, cell phone, internet service, newspaper, heat, electric, house alarm, groceries, clothing, gas for car, health care, and taxes. The point...enjoy college.

338. Resist the urge to always have your cell phone.

339. If you do have a cell phone, resist the urge to upgrade every time some new gadget comes out.

340. The best time in college to start looking for a job after you graduate is freshmen year.

341. Become friendly with your schools career guidance person.

342. If you have the chance to live on the water while in college, do so!

343. Don't forget to thank your sports information director.

344. Don't bite your fingernails.

345. Read on the stairmaster.

346. Play racquetball.

347. Drive slower.

348. Pick a goal, make a fun bet on the outcome with a teammate.

349. Vote: On campus and in public elections

350. Watch movies without violence.

351. Give to the make-a-wish foundation.

352. Thank your sports maintenance staff.

353. Make a pregame cd with the favorite music of the seniors.

354. Never cheat on a paper or exam.

355. Every once in a while, hand write a letter instead of an email.

356. Take off your sunglasses when meeting someone new. Look them in the eye.

357. Always buy any of the dollar fundraisers going on on campus.

358. Always remember, you are a customer of the school. Your tax dollars or tuition pay the salary of the employees. This means you should get good customer service.

359. While each situation is different, college is really too early a time to get married and/or have children.

360. Wear a watch, be on time, but don't be obsessed by time.

361. If you win a championship ring, order it in your one of your parents size and give it to them.

362. Freshmen year live in the freshmen dorms. Sophomore and junior year, work your way up to the nicest dorms. Senior year, live in an apartment off campus, it is a good adjustment to real life.

363. The best part of cafeteria food, as you will appreciate later in life, is that you do not have to shop for groceries, put them away, cook, and then do the dishes.

364. Many supplements sold over the counter are illegal with the NCAA. Make sure you know what you are taking and that it is safe and also approved by the NCAA.

365. Thank your bus driver.

366. Being a residence advisor (RA) can save you a ton of money off your college bill.

367. Informational interviewing, will always
be the best way to get a job in any field.

368. Almost everyone would benefit from
seeing a counselor.

369. Control your temper.

370. Soon enough there are no tomorrows.

371. Don't confuse today with yesterday or
tomorrow.

372. Play the game the right way.

373. Be a "ballplayer."

374. Foster an environment of teamwork.

375. Your team is your family.

376. Problems are opportunities.

377. You are what you do. How much effort you give, reveals who you are.

378. Excellence is an all the time thing.

379. Don't guess your future, make it.

380. No risk, no reward.

381. The Grand Canyon was built by the perseverance of water.

382. It usually takes thousands of hours of preparation for moments of success.

383. Know your limits. Then go past them.

384. Some try to keep the customer happy. Others keep the workers so happy, it rubs off on the customers.

385. "Watch your thoughts, for they become words. Choose your words, for they become actions. Understand your actions, for they become habits. Study your habits, for they will become your character. Develop your character, for it becomes your destiny."

386. DIMITT! Determination is more important than talent.

387. Is the thing in your way an obstacle or something you can step on to move higher?

388. Live your dream.

389. Water is free, but worth its weight in gold for athletes.

390. During two a day practices in the heat, water is your best friend and lifeline.

391. Those that are bored, often find trouble to get into.

392. Those that love what the sport they play, will never think of it as work.

393. In baseball it is "play ball", not "work ball."

394. Don't stop when practice ends.

395. Dress like an athlete on the field, like a student in the classroom.

396. Take every opportunity to learn something new from your coach, a new position, drill, skill, etc.

397. Hard work is more important than talent.

398. Give you coach more then he expects,
all with a smile on your face.

399. Just telling a teammate how much they
mean and what a good job they are
doing can go a long way.

400. Enthusiasm for life will go a long way
towards your success on the field and
off it.

401. Even if you quit the team, stay on good terms with the coaches and players.

402. They key to college life, with all its choices, is to figure out what matters to you and spend most of your time doing that.

403. Time relaxing is not enjoyed unless you worked for it.

404. Have short term and long-term goals.

405. Everything can be done better.

406. Don't think you miss practice or the team, try going without them for a while.

407. Leave things better then you find them.

408. Drive safe.

409. Watch a sunrise.

410. If you like your results, stay the course, if not, switch it up.

411. Five minutes early is on time.

412. Equipment does not make up for talent.

413. When given a difficult task, finish it.

414. Make sure you have an extra car key and a way to get into your dorm if you lose your key.

415. There is greatness within each of you. Seeds turn into giant trees.

416. Treat the planet like it is something you have paid for because you have.

417. Perseverance. Fail thirty times, succeed on the thirty-first.

418. Peace is often harder then war.

419. Regardless of how you feel, always try to act like a winner. Soon you will feel like you act.

420. Always have a victory speech.

421. Choose a college for the school, not just to coach or the team.

422. If you want to play sports in college, take time to figure out the right level for you.

423. Learn how to market yourself to college coaches. Pepsi markets their soda…how do they do?

424. Confused on which college to attend, spend the night.

425. When there is competition at stake, there are no shortcuts.

426. Most people who are one hundred per-cent, truly satisfied, are often failures.

427. A lot of things are more important then sports...when you figure them out, let me know.

428. Throw strikes, until home plate moves, there are no excuses.

429. Lying spreads quickly, but the truth will always be around.

430. Often you can learn from your team-mates bad examples.

431. Practice when you practice and rest when you rest.

432. Experience is when you take the test first and then get the lesson afterward.

433. Play for the games sake.

434. Sprinters train so very hard for ten seconds of competition.

435. Most sports require intense concentration and effort for six seconds with breaks in between.

436. Invest in a good mattress and sheets.

437. If you don't think what you do off the field effects what you do on it, you are as wrong as can be.

438. Commit yourself to getting bigger, stronger, faster, and quicker.

439. College athletes need laptops.

440. Learn when to multitask and when to focus on one thing.

441. You must raise up to meet success.

442. Concern yourself only with what you can control.

443. Email is great, but use a phone or go in person when you want something done.

444. Flow of the game sports (basketball, football) are often less nerve-racking on the players then mechanical (tennis, golf, baseball) sports.

445. If you don't think you play the game against the ball (or puck, etc) try playing without it.

446. Breathe in through the nose, out through the mouth.

447. If you want your coach to let you do big things, first show him you can do small things.

448. Resist the urge to drive fast on campus.

449. Just do something…even a walk beats sitting on the couch.

450. Park far away from where you are going.

451. Take the stairs.

452. Travel with a jump rope.

453. If you need to memorize anything, try it while walking.

454. Play intramurals or in a recreational league.

455. Don't fall for fad diets or exercises.

456. Be a fan of pro players, but be your own hero.

457. Save money, drink tap water.

458. Protein bars and shakes are better then most other snacks and also beat skipping meals.

459. Gambling is a waste of your time and money. It is also illegal for college athletes.

460. Always send your mom a card on Valentine's Day.

461. Having problems beats being dead.

462. Your health is more most important skill.

463. If you ever find yourself bored, start a small sports niche company. For example, buy wood baseball bats and add artwork to personalize them.

464. The Under Armour company was started by a college senior.

465. Work a youth camp if you get the chance.

466. Be a gamer.

467. If you want more responsibility do all the little things right.

468. Watch Caddy-shack and Slap Shot.

469. In any company or team, good people are the most important asset.

470. "The Devil finds work for idle hands."

471. Don't think that a B.A. ,B.S, M.A, M.D, or Ph.D. is the only way to success. Motivation and self-learning are just as important.

472. Always stand and be respectful for the national anthem.

473. Excellence is a habit.

474. The worst mistake is the one you don't learn from.

475. Your team will be much better when no one cares who gets the credit.

476. No one can control your dreams.

477. Mark Twain said, "I never let schooling interfere with my education.

478. A diamond was once a piece of coal.

479. Life is all perspective. Inmates at Alcatraz hated to be fed lobster.

480. Your ability to improve at your sport, starts with an open mind.

481. Find a mentor.

482. Study statistics, but don't be at their mercy.

483. Trust your instincts in the game.

484. When it comes to getting recruited by college coaches, unless you are a super-star, prepare yourself to recruit the coach. Market yourself.

485. Register for the NCAA Clearinghouse.

486. A boss tells you to do something, a leader does it with you.

487. Don't think of sports as you vs. them. It is really you vs. you.

488. A beautiful flower takes time to bloom. You can't plant a seed and expect a flower the next day.

489. Your key in life is to find out what your goal is and then to create actions and habits that constantly lead to that goal.

490. If you had to pick what would you choose, a great car and house, or inner peace?

491. Practice is not only the learning of new skills, but keeping your skills at the ready.

492. Even dogs love sports.

493. If you would rather win ugly against an overmatched opponent, then play well and lose a close one against a great team, you are not in the sport for the right reason.

494. Control your anger, one moment of a lost temper can cost you so much more.

495. Your health is way more important then being in shape.

496. This is what I know about steroids…if you take them you are a tremendous idiot.

497. Love is great. Sports are great. One should never rule out the other, rather they both can be part of your life.

498. Give and you get.

499. Buy a mini iPod.

500. Go all out or just go home.

Other Projects by Wayne Mazzoni

The Athletic Recruiting and Scholarship Guide. Also on CD and VHS.

You vs. You: Sport Psychology for Life

The Left-Handed Pick Off Move.

For additional copies of the book, including quantity discounts, visit
www.WayneMazzoni.com
or email Wayne@waynemazzoni.com

If you have any original quotes you would like to share, please forward them to
Wayne@waynemazzoni.com